Understanding Shodokan Aikido

Basics through 7th Kyu

SP
U S A

Understanding Shodokan Aikido

Basics through 7th Kyu

by Sean Masaki Flynn

Japan Aikido Association/USA

Shodokan Publishing USA

Published by Shodokan Publishing USA

Design and typeset by Bud Zehmer, WhorledPeas

Photos © 2000 Kerry Nettles

Library of Congress Cataloging-in-Publication Applied For.

ISBN 0-9647083-1-0

Printed by QUESTprint

Disclaimer

All material included in this book or reproduced or repeated elsewhere by or in any medium whatsoever is intended for educational purposes only. Both the author and Shodokan Publishing USA give notice that the techniques presented in this work are dangerous and that injury or death can result from their application, whether performed correctly or incorrectly. No warrantee or guarantee as to the safety or efficacy of the martial arts techniques presented in this book is made, either explicitly or implicitly. The practice of the techniques in this book should only be performed under the supervision of a professional martial arts instructor, and then only after consultation with a physician. Application of some or all of the techniques described in this book may be prohibited in some or all situations under local, state, or federal law. No representations are made by the author or Shodokan Publishing USA regarding the appropriateness or legality of the use of the techniques presented in this book.

Shodokan Publishing USA
5752 S Kingston Way
Englewood, CO 80111

Table of Contents

Dedication

To the living legacy of Kenji Tomiki and Hideo Ohba, who through the development of Sport Aikido gave Aikido practitioners everywhere a new and vigorous way to hone their skills, focus their minds, and open their hearts.

Also to Tetsuro Nariyama, Fumiaki Shishida, Kenshi Uno, and the current generation of instructors both Japanese and gaijin who have worked so hard to spread Shodokan Aikido to every inhabited continent so that thousands can now benefit from the ideas and ideals of Tomiki and Ohba.

And to my mother and mothers everywhere, who teach us the Aiki of living.

Introduction

Kenji Tomiki was blessed to be born in the year that he was. Had he been born much sooner, he would likely never have become a top student of Morihei Ueshiba; and had be been born much later, he would never have had the chance to study under Jigoro Kano. Being born in 1901, he was able to not only study Aikido and Judo, but to study them as a direct student of their respective founders, Ueshiba and Kano.

That he studied both, and both under their founders, is crucial to understanding the contributions that he was to make to both Aikido and Judo. From the Aikido and Daito-ryu aiki-jujutsu that he learned from Ueshiba, Tomiki was to make for Kodokan Judo its Goshin Jutsu (Self-Defense) kata, which remains to this day a testing requirement for Judo black belts. From what he had learned from Kano, Tomiki was to develop for Aikido both sparring and competition systems which Aikido practitioners can use to hone their skills. Professor Tomiki frequently related how fortunate he was to receive direct training from both of these extremely gifted teachers. As he once said, "I learned the true meaning of really profound martial arts skills and techniques from Ueshiba, and I learned the doctrines, innovations and educational merits of the martial arts from Kano Sensei."

In April of 1958, the first month of the Japanese academic calendar, Tomiki Sensei took several of his top Judo students at Waseda University and used them to form an Aikido Club at that institution. At the time, Tomiki was both a Professor at Waseda University and an instructor at the Kodokan (the world Judo Headquarters). When he first approached the university with his idea about starting an Aikido club, the school was hesitant. The directors of the university dictated that to receive official sanction and school support, Tomiki would have to set up the club in such a way that there would be objective measures of student progress. This suited Tomiki just fine. The way that objective progress was measured in Judo, Kendo, and Karate was through the use of tournaments whereby not only outsiders but club members themselves could gauge the efficacy of what their sensei was teaching them. Since Tomiki desired to use the club as an experimental group to develop sparring and competition methods for Aikido, the university's requirement was effortlessly accommodated.

By 1958, Ueshiba had been teaching Aikido and Aiki-jujutsu for over 30 years. Most of his early students, like Tomiki, had had extensive experience with competitive martial arts such as Judo, Kendo, or Sumo. As such, these early students had a very good idea of the difficulties of dealing with a fully resisting opponent. Tomiki was afraid, however, that the later students of Aikido, most of whom had little competitive experience and who were trained exclusively in kata (forms), would not be able to apply Aikido techniques effectively against equally well-trained opponents. If those opponents were resisting fully and counter-attacking using their full will power and arsenal of skill and knowledge, Tomiki feared that kata-only training would prove ineffective. It was to give Aikido practitioners a safe sparring system by which to test and improve their technique and their mettle that Tomiki set up the Waseda University Aikido Club in April, 1958.

However, Tomiki's reasons for wishing to introduce sparring and competition to Aikido went further than just the improvement of technique. Tomiki shared Kano's vision that competitive martial arts could be used to teach mutual respect, sportsmanship, endurance, humility, patience, courtesy, creativity, determination, calmness, courage, alertness and a host of other virtues which would make for not only better martial artists but for better human beings.

Furthermore, Tomiki saw himself as an educator, not a pedant. At the time that he started that first Aikido club, a good deal of Japanese martial arts was being handed down in the tradition way, in which masters were always presumed to be right about everything. The consequence of that mindset was that students were expected to exactly duplicate their sensei's every movement and never think about building upon or expanding or personalizing their training. Tomiki, however, encouraged his students to develop their own applications and techniques as long as they remembered to rest their new creations on the basic fundamental principles of Aikido. Tomiki firmly believed that once a student had been properly taught the basic methods and principals, that student—and that student's martial arts and human development—could grow without limit.

It was for this reason that Tomiki gave the name "Shodokan" to the dojo that he founded to be the headquarters of the style of Aikido that he developed over the last 20 years of his life. Shodokan means "The House of the Enlightened Way." Translated into English, that name can seem to indicate that Tomiki felt that he had discovered the one true Enlightened Way and that his dojo was to serve as a vehicle to disseminate his system. But that would be a mistranslation. What Tomiki intended was for his dojo to be a place where students from all over the world could come together and discover for themselves and for each other new innovations that would help all of them to progress along the Enlightened Way. His Shodokan Dojo was intended as a place for them to meet, and for Aikido to continue to develop and grow for the betterment of all.

It is the hope of the members of the Japan Aikido Association (USA) that this book and forthcoming books in this series will help to introduce the basics and fundamentals of Aikido to many people in the English speaking world. In that way, we will be furthering Tomiki Sensei's belief that once the basics are learned, students can go grow without limitations. To see as many people as possible grow as much as possible through the instrument of Aikido would go some way to paying back Ueshiba and Tomiki Senseis for the gift that they have given us, and for which we are very grateful.

Basic Principles of Aikido Techniques

Aikido is a martial art with a deep and comprehensive theory. This theory is both philosophical and physical, addressing both the profound moral questions as to *when* and *why* one should fight, as well as the technical details of *how* one should fight. For many forms of martial arts, the how of the style and the matter of the why and when one should fight are not woven together very tightly. In the case of Aikido, however, these strands of the art cannot be separated. The techniques used, the how, have been chosen specifically to conform completely to the moral philosophy of Aikido, which details the why and the when of fighting. So, before we begin our study of the how of Aikido, we must delve into its why and when, which have as their base a strongly held humanistic philosophy.

Aikido perceives the attacker as one who has fallen out of harmony with the universe and self.

This humanistic philosophy has earned Aikido great renown and great popularity. The basic moral principle of Aikido is that one should not view an attacker as someone to whom anything can be justifiably done in self defense, but rather as a wayward soul whom one should help to once again walk the right path. That is, Aikido does not perceive the attacker as some sort of "bad person" to whom one can justifiably respond with great violence. Rather, he is seen as a basically decent fellow who has sadly fallen out of harmony with the universe and himself, and who should therefore be subdued, calmed down, and talked to until he realizes the error of his ways.

This charitable view of the attacker constrains the how of one's defense. For if the attacker is not a bad guy to whom one can justifiably do anything, then one has to moderate one's defenses. Consequently, the techniques of Aikido emphasize non-injurious submission holds and pins, so that the attack can be neutralized without harming the attacker. As a measure of the effectiveness of Aikido techniques in achieving this goal of defending without causing harm, it should be noted that a great number of Aikido techniques have been adopted by police forces around the world precisely because police officers are under a legal obligation to take criminals into custody without harming them unless absolutely necessary.

The how of Aikido is more elaborate, though, than just choosing techniques based upon the criterion that they not hurt the attacker. Even in *kote-gaeshi*, a common and standard Aikido technique, the sequence of moves involved is extremely complicated. Indeed, high levels of complexity are common to virtually all Aikido techniques. This complexity could be dealt with by teaching each technique in isolation and in great detail. However, it was noted long ago that several things—good posture, proper movement, and correct timing—were common to all techniques. That being the case, the student's ability to absorb new techniques and progress quickly is greatly improved if he or she is taught each new technique in light of how it incorporates those things common to all techniques. By teaching in such a manner, each new technique reinforces the principles present in all.

Several skills, for instance proper eye contact with the opponent and the maintenance of proper distance from him, are also needed to effectively utilize Aikido in a confrontation. While these skills are separate from techniques per se, they too can be treated as common skills to be employed by the practitioner while performing Aikido. It is the elaboration and systematization of these many commonalties that gives the technical, physical side of the theory of Aikido its utility and profundity. Thus, it is now to the more important of these common factors that we turn, as a proper understanding of each factor will aid the student in both the comprehension of Aikido and the execution of Aikido techniques.

Aikido is a defensive martial art not only because its practitioner tries not to harm the attacker, but because the attacker is normally allowed to attack first. Waiting for an attack to develop gives a tactical advantage to the defender. Although the opponent gets to move first, the defender can use that first motion against the attacker. Aikido does not hold to the football maxim that the best defense is a strong offense. Rather, it takes advantage of the strategic fact that in a situation where the defender has not been surprised, he is at an advantage relative to the attacker because the attacker has to come at someone who is prepared to defend. As any military strategist (or any World War I veteran) will tell you, one never wants to attack a prepared defender. Rather, the best position for an attacker is to try to catch the opponent or victim unaware and overwhelm him before he can coordinate a defense. It was for this reason that the Germans developed blitzkrieg, lightning warfare, in World War II to avoid the futile attacks against prepared defenses that were such a major feature of World War I. In the same way, a mugger or a thug will always try to overwhelm his or her victim before the victim can mount a defense.

Attacking the prepared is dangerous for two reasons. First, if you attack someone who is prepared to defend, then you may well be hurt or killed by the defender. Second, and a reason more subtle and central to Aikido, there is always an element of commitment on the part of the attacker. Aikido thrives on taking advantage of that commitment.

For instance, imagine someone taking a step toward you and swinging a baseball bat at you. Though this may take only a half-second or so, bats are heavy, and once a full swing is initiated, that swing cannot be readily stopped or redirected. Because of this, you are presented with a great opportunity. If you can avoid being hit by the bat, you have before you an opponent who, by swinging a bat full force, has rendered himself completely committed to that attack for as long as it takes to finish it. His arms are both busy holding the bat, so he can't use them to punch or block or grab. His feet must remain firmly planted on the ground so that the momentum of the swing doesn't throw him off balance; therefore he can't use them to kick or block. Indeed, his whole body is committed to the big swing; no part of his body can be used for defense until that big swing is completed.

Aikido takes advantage of this commitment by executing techniques against the opponent while the opponent is preoccupied with finishing his attack. Of course, this tactic of defending only after the opponent has attacked can only be done if one lets the opponent make the first move. However, what if the first attack works? What if that big swing takes your head off?

It is this very real problem with letting the attacker move first that the theory of Aikido first addresses. Aikido's solution to the problem can be divided into three concepts. The first is *shizen-tai,* or natural posture. The second is *ma-ai,* or proper distance between attacker and defender. The third is *me-tsuke,* or proper eye contact in the fight situation. As will be explained in the sections below, the Aikido practitioner properly utilizing these three concepts will eliminate the danger of letting the attacker attack first, as they all work together to render the attack very unlikely to succeed.

Anticipation and Preparation

Shizen-tai

Shizen-tai is Japanese for natural posture. In Aikido, it refers to a very specific stance that one should take when one senses a threat. As can be seen in Figures 1 and 2, shizen-tai involves standing with the feet parallel and shoulder width apart, the knees slightly bent, the back straight, and the arms relaxed at the side, so that one's weight is equally distributed between the two feet, and rests mostly on the balls of the feet. The heels should be lightly touching the ground.

Note several things about this stance. First, the feet really must be parallel and must be pointing directly forward. This placement forces body weight onto the balls of the feet, preparing one to move even before any attack is made. Having the weight on the balls of the feet facilitates quick movement, as whenever one moves, one has to push one's body weight around by the balls of the feet. To see the limitations of other stances, try standing with your knees locked and with your weight on your heels. From that stance, it is very hard to move quickly, as one must first bend the knees and ankles, put weight onto the balls of the feet, tense one's muscles, and then

Figure 1 & 2

合氣道

push off. Each of those actions takes precious time. Standing in shizen-tai makes sure that they are all done well before any attack has to be dealt with. Standing with the feet parallel and with the knees already bent means that you are prepared to move; your weight is on the balls of the feet, and your muscles are tensed and ready to go. The attacker will not succeed just by catching you off guard.

Next, note that shizen-tai is done with the back straight and the arms relaxed at the sides. A person standing straight up can move greater distances faster than a person in a squatting stance. Compare the shizen-tai stance with Sumo wrestling's *jigo-tai*, a crouched defensive stance. Jigo-tai is good for holding one's ground and pushing really hard, but it renders quick movements over more than a couple of feet impossible. Since Aikido requires quick movements over several feet to get out of the way of initial attacks, the upright and mobile posture of shizen-tai is called for.

Finally, note that neither foot is forward. Standing with either of the feet forward limits one's mobility and therefore how one can defend against any given attack. Worse, that limitation is clearly visible to the attacker, who can see very clearly which of your legs is forward, and so in which directions your mobility is limited. Standing with either of the legs forward also has a tendency to give away the important information as to whether you are right-handed or left-handed. Because of these disadvantages, Shodokan Aikido emphasizes the shizen-tai stance, wherein no limitations are made upon the direction of movement of the defender, and consequently no informational advantage is given to the attacker.

As the feet do not give away any information, so the arms dangle naturally at the sides. The arms down, the attacker has no idea as to whether you are right-handed or left-handed. He also has no idea whether you have studied boxing, in which case you would be standing with your arms up high and your fists clenched; or karate, in which case you would likely be standing with your arms held mid-level, with your hands either in fists or stiff with the fingers extended; or grappling, in which case your arms would be held high, with the hands loose and the fingers pointing out at the attacker ready to grab him. If he were able to ascertain by looking at you what fighting skills you likely possess, he could modify his attack appropriately, by aiming, for example, to grapple with the boxer or to strike from a distance at the grappler. But with the arms dangling loosely at the sides, he knows nothing about your training. Better yet, he may go so far as to concluded incorrectly that you have no martial arts training and are therefore an easy mark. That overconfidence can work to your advantage.

Ma-ai

Ma-ai is the Japanese term for proper distance. Ma-ai is what makes the tactic of letting the attacker attack first a tenable strategy, for it allows the defender enough time and space so that the attacker is not likely to succeed with his initial onslaught. The Japanese characters for ma-ai literally mean the "interval of meeting" and refer to how close the attacker and defender stand from each other when a fight begins. In Aikido, this interval is defined as the distance the opponents stand from each other when, while standing erect, they are just able to touch weapon tips. For two unarmed opponents, the weapons in question are their hands, and so ma-ai is the distance they stand from each other when they are just able to reach out their arms and touch fingertips. This is illustrated in Figure 3. For two opponents with swords, ma-ai is the distance they stand from each other when they are just able to touch their sword tips together. This is illustrated in Figure 4. If one opponent has a weapon and the other is unarmed, ma-ai is still the distance from weapon tip to weapon tip, the unarmed man's weapon being his hands. Such a situation is illustrated in Figure 5.

This particular distance was chosen to be the proper distance for a simple reason. If two people are at ma-ai, then in order for one to attack, he must first take a step forward. Without stepping forward, he cannot come into contact with the other person, no matter how much he leans forward or tries to extend a punching arm, a kicking leg, or a swinging sword.

Without taking a step forward, the distance of ma-ai cannot be covered. Therefore, in order for an attack to be successful, a step must be taken forward. The time involved in taking that step, however, allows the defender to formulate a defense. That defense can be as simple as stepping backward so as to reestablish ma-ai. Or, depending on the attack, it can involve closing with the opponent and applying a technique. One should never get into a reflex contest with a stranger, and the maintenance of ma-ai means that one never has to rely on one's own reflexes being faster than an opponent's. The time the attacker must take to cover the ma-ai distance allows the defender plenty of time to react and defend, even if the attacker is inherently quicker than the defender.

Ma-ai also serves to force the opponent to make a committed attack. Taking a step forward to attack means that a committed action is made by the attacker. As explained above, defenders can take advantage of such committed acts. Hence,

Figure 3–5

ma-ai is helpful not only in giving the defender time to formulate a defense, but also in giving him a physically committed opponent against whom to defend. Both, of course, make defending much easier.

Finally, it is up to the defender to ensure that ma-ai is achieved. He must keep the attacker at proper distance, as the attacker will wish to move in closer so that he may launch an attack from such a proximity that the defender will not be able to effectively respond. Students of aikido should be sure to begin all techniques from ma-ai distance.

Me-tsuke

The Japanese meaning of *me-tsuke* is literally to put one's eyes on something. At one time it referred to the government spies who helped to keep the people of feudal Japan in line. In modern Aikido usage, me-tsuke refers to the proper way of maintaining eye contact with an opponent. Done properly, me-tsuke involves keeping one's eyes always upon those of the opponent. However, it does not mean that one is concentrating on or staring at the opponent's eyes. Rather, one should be mentally aware of everything that is in the field of vision. Though the center of one's gaze is upon the opponent's eyes, one is clearly discerning every punch, every kick, and every twitching finger.

Me-tsuke is done this way in Aikido for several reasons. First, the eyes are the gateway to the soul; very often an attacker will indicate his intentions by an unconscious glance at his intended target. Second, keeping the center of one's gaze upon the opponent's eyes allows one to take advantage of the fact that one's reaction time when seeing an action using peripheral vision is less than one's reaction time when one sees that same action while staring directly at it. When one actively stares at and examines something, the nervous system relays all that visual information to the higher brain where it is rather slowly processed. Visual signals caught out of the corner of the eye, however, are only passed along to the lower-level brain. This part of the brain is in charge of reflex action, so that things you see in peripheral vision are responded to by the lightning-quick, reflexive part of the brain. Me-tsuke takes advantage of this fact about how our brains process visual information. By keeping one's eyes on the opponent's, one leaves the opponent's legs, arms and torso, the dangerous parts of his body, in the area covered by peripheral vision. Therefore, any movements in those dangerous body parts will trigger reflexively quick responses on the part of the nervous system. With proper training in the martial arts, those quick, reflexive responses will be appropriate and effective.

Finally, me-tsuke prevents one from getting into the bad habit of fixating on one single thing during a fight and ignoring other things that might be very important. This is true even before an attack has been initiated. If one stares at the knife in an assailant's hand, one's mind will likely become fixated upon that weapon. As a result, the assailant may be able to launch a kick to the head without it being noticed until it's too late. Such fixation is also a problem after an assailant has attacked and during a counterattack. For example, most Aikido techniques involve rather complex manipulations of the opponent's joints. It is tempting to stare at one's own hands as they go through the motions necessary to complete a technique. However, doing so is harmful because, among other reasons, one's concentration has a tendency to follow one's vision, so that one will not notice until it is too late that the opponent is counterattacking. By keeping the center of one's field of vision upon the opponent's eyes, all visual information is treated equally. This helps to greatly mitigate the tendency to fixate mentally on any one thing, fixation being a weakness that a savvy opponent will exploit.

The Interrelationship of Shizen-tai, Ma-ai, and Me-tsuke

Before we go on to discuss other unifying fundamentals of Aikido, let us pause to look at the interrelationship between shizen-tai, ma-ai, and me-tsuke. All three are needed to ensure that a defender attempting to use the Aikido strategy of letting the attacker attack first will survive such a strategy and be in a position to respond effectively. Shizen-tai ensures that the defender is prepared to move quickly and over a large distance. Keeping proper distance, ma-ai, ensures that the defender will have enough time to formulate a defense and won't be engaged in a battle of reflexes with the attacker. Proper eye contact, me-tsuke, helps the defender to move faster than he otherwise would by exploiting peripheral vision and reflexive action. It also prevents him from fixating on any one particular thing during an engagement. For effective Aikido, practitioners must ensure that they have good posture, keep the attacker at proper distance, and are utilizing me-tsuke to view the developing situation.

Reaction

There are several other principles that underpin the proper execution of all Aikido techniques. The three mentioned previously are important throughout a fight, but must be performed even *before* the first attack is made. Conversely, the ones that follow deal with the period *after* the attack has begun, while a defense is being initiated. Like the previous three, those that follow are crucial and should be understood well.

Tai-sabaki

Tai-sabaki is the Japanese term for body evasion. It refers to getting out of the way of an attack. It is important because Aikido never meets force with force. In Aikido, unlike in most of the striking arts, one never blocks a punch with a forearm or puts up a shin to stop a roundhouse kick. In Aikido, one simply gets out of the way.

This is done for several reasons. Among them is the fact that getting hit can be very dangerous, even if one manages to block with proper form and in the nick of time. But the crucial reason that Aikido dictates getting out of the way is that doing so allows the defender to take advantage of the interval of commitment that accompanies every strike. This interval of

Figures 6–9

commitment arises because strikes take time to complete. If one gets out of the way before the strike is finished, one can do things to the attacker while he is stuck finishing his strike. If, instead, one were to stand one's ground, not move out of the way, and perform a block, then one would give up the opportunity to take advantage of the interval of commitment. By the time the block is completed, the attack is also completed and the interval of commitment is past.

Worse, after the exchange of a strike and a block, the attacker will likely be closer than ma-ai, so that his next strike will land unless he is exceptionally slow or the defender is exceptionally quick. Holding one's ground and blocking just leads to a prolonged exchange of strikes, or to being thrown to the ground by someone who knows grappling.

In Figures 6-7, an unarmed opponent performs a tai-sabaki by simply moving to his left to avoid the falling sword. In Figures 8-9, the same unarmed opponent performs a different tai-sabaki, this time moving forward as well as to his left. This second tai-sabaki brings him close to the attacker. Generally, the tai-sabaki undertaken will depend not only on the attack made but also on the technique that the defender wishes to perform subsequently. As one learns new Aikido techniques, one gets a sense of the tai-sabaki needed to place oneself in a position to properly perform each technique.

Sei-chu sen

When one is executing an Aikido technique, one should always make sure that the technique is done in front of one's own sei-chu sen. *Sei-chu sen* refers to one's center line. This imaginary line bisects the body from the top of the head down to the groin. To find the location of your center line, place your palms together as if in prayer. While keeping them pressed together, raise them up and down vertically, as in

Figures 10–12

Figures 10-12. As you can see, the palms always stay in front of the center line.

The hands should be kept in front of the center line while doing techniques because one can push with far more force against things that are in one's center than against things that are to one's side. It is also far easier to twist someone's wrist if one's hands are in one's center. If you ever find yourself having to use a great deal of upper body strength to perform a technique, quickly check to see if you are doing the technique with your hands properly in your center. If you are using a lot of strength, chances are that your hands are off your center line.

Ido-ryoku

Ido-ryoku refers to locomotive power, or the power of movement. Specifically, it describes the power generated when one moves one's center around. *One's center* is defined as one's center of mass, the point around which the body would balance if it were placed on a fulcrum. For almost all people, the center of mass is in the middle of the belly, just below the navel.

To push from one's center is to push with the whole body and not just with an arm. This difference is very important

Figures 13–14

合氣道

because of the limitations of the arm, both in terms of the distance over which it can push, as well as the amount of force with which it can push. By both measurements, pushing with the arm is far less effective than pushing with the center. If one does not step forward, the farthest distance that one can push an object is limited by arm length, and how much strength one can push with is limited to how strong the arm is. On the other hand, if one pushes from the center, then one can push as far as the legs will carry the body, and one can push utilizing the full force of body momentum, which is limited only by mass and speed.

To see the difference in distance between pushing with the arm and pushing with the center, look closely at Figures 13-14 and 15-17. In Figures 13-14, pushing is done just with the arm. The legs are not moved. Note that extension is not very far, as it is limited by the length of the arm. Further, power is limited by the strength of the arm doing the pushing. Pushing this way is not very effective.

To see the correct way to

Figures 15–17

push, look at Figures 15-17, where pushing is done with the center. The arm starts out fully extended and stays that way during the push, which is executed by moving the feet and carrying the whole body forward. Force is provided by body momentum. As you can see, a much greater distance can be covered and a great deal more force applied than when pushing with just the arm.

The proper way to utilize ido-ryoku is to think of always moving from the center of mass. Think of transferring the energy of one's moving center through one's arms and into the thing or person being pushed. Never try to utilize pure upper body or arm strength in Aikido. Doing so is a bad habit that prevents one from utilizing the much greater power of ido-ryoku.

Kuzushi

Kuzushi is Japanese for breaking balance. It is the use of kuzushi in every technique that allows Aikido to do away with punches and kicks and yet still be an effective martial art. Through the use of kuzushi, the weak can successfully utilize Aikido against the strong. One must pay a great deal of attention to kuzushi and how it is achieved if one wants to practice good Aikido.

To see the need for kuzushi in Aikido, note that while defending against an attack, the following sequence of events almost always takes place. First, one is at ma-ai waiting for the attack. Second, the attack is made. Then, one performs tai-sabaki to avoid the attack and get into position to perform a technique. Next, before the attacker has finished his attack, the defender begins a technique by using some form of kuzushi to push the attacker off balance. Finally, while the attacker is off balance and attempting to right himself, the defender completes the technique.

From beginning to end, Aikido attempts to never give the attacker a second chance. The attacker does get to attack first, but the defender takes advantage of the attacker's commitment to avoid the attack with tai-sabaki. Then, before the attacker can respond to the fact that his attack has failed, the defender has already begun to push the attacker off balance with kuzushi. Finally, before the attacker can regain his broken balance, the defender has finished applying an Aikido technique to the attacker. After the attack begins, the attacker is always kept one step behind events and remains totally off balance mentally and physically.

Kuzushi is key to this process. If one just plays tai-sabaki and avoids the initial attack, not only will the attacker reestablish his balance, he will also have likely moved close enough to do some harm. To prevent this, the defender must not only perform tai-sabaki but must immediately follow it up by getting and maintaining kuzushi.

Further, none of the techniques of Aikido work well unless preceded by kuzushi. Wrist locks, arm bars, and throws are all effortless if they are done after having broken the attacker's balance. They are nearly impossible otherwise. Therefore, even if tai-sabaki is successful, the defender cannot go directly to the application of a technique. He must first break the attacker's balance. If he does so, then not only will the technique be easy to apply but the attacker will also be too unsteady to frustrate the technique or harm the defender while the technique is being completed.

To see how tai-sabaki and kuzushi work together, look at Figures 18-21. Here the defender performs a tai-sabaki, which takes him forward and to his left (Figures 18–19). Doing so leaves him in an excellent position to utilize the momentum of the attacker's falling sword against the attacker, and throw him off balance (Figure 20) by pushing down on the sword hilt farther than the attacker would have liked. Theswordsman is kept off balance by being pushed down (Figure 21) and to the side. With his balance so completely broken, he is an easy target for an Aikido technique.

Attacking the Body's Weak Points

Rather than applying overwhelming strength, Aikido prefers minimal strength applied while the attacker is unable to effectively respond, either due to the commitment inherent in his attack, or due to the application of kuzushi to render him off-balance. Additionally, Aikido exploits the weak points of the human body, thereby greatly reducing the need for bodily strength or size when dealing with an attacker.

The bodily weak points that Aikido most often attacks are the joints. Aikido encompasses hundreds of techniques designed to work against the joints of the hands, arms, shoulders, and neck. Whereas one would have to hit a strong attacker very hard in the chest to end a fight, Aikido can be used effectively without employing much force. A relatively small amount of force when skillfully applied can lock up even a strong attacker's wrist, put him in a world of pain, and immobilize him. Joint locks are also great ways of achieving kuzushi: many techniques begin

Figures 18–21

with a joint-lock kuzushi to break the attacker's balance.

The human body is also weak in other exploitable ways. Our bodies have only two legs, which are sometimes hard to utilize. Just to stand up straight and still, the brain has to make dozens of fine muscular adjustments throughout the body every second. As a result, in the fluid situation of a fight, it is relatively easy to overwhelm the brain's ability to make adjustments quickly enough to keep a person standing. Aikido exploits this in many of its throws by leaning the attacker over too quickly for him to regain his balance. Another bodily weakness is the inability of the legs to step in certain directions. This too is exploited by certain Aikido techniques, and can be seen in Figures 18–21, where after kuzushi is applied in Figure 20, the swordsman is pushed sideways in Figure 21. This puts all of his weight onto his right foot, leaning him over. Worse for him, in the direction in which he is being pushed, it is impossible for him to use his left foot to make a recovery quickly enough to do him any good. He must either release the sword or fall.

Timing

Perhaps the most subtle skill common to all techniques in Aikido is timing. Proper timing is needed to know when to move out of the way of an attack. It is needed when deciding when to begin a kuzushi action. It is needed when deciding to move from the kuzushi portion of a technique to the technique's finish. Timing is very complicated and can only be learned through regular practice. Let it just be said here that the student should know that moving too early is as bad as moving too late, and that the timing needed to perform the same technique against different people will necessarily vary due to each person's unique speed, strength, size, and aggressiveness. The student should learn to modify his timing to each attacker and each situation.

The student of Aikido should understand three basic concepts with regard to the timing of attack and defense. These are *go-no-sen, ai-uchi,* and *sen-sen-no-sen*. The Aikido practitioner normally waits for an attack to proceed for some time before responding. This corresponds to the concept of *go-no-sen,* or moving after an attack. Aikido does, however, allow for beginning a defense simultaneous to the beginning of an attack. This is known as *ai-uchi,* or closing simultaneously with the opponent. Finally, it is also possible for the Aikido practitioner to precipitate an attack, thereby undertaking *sen-sen-no-sen.* Precipitating an attack does not mean throwing a sucker punch or merely moving first. Rather, the term conveys the possession of such a deep mental control over an opponent that you lure him into moving in the direction that you desire, often without his even being aware that you manipulate him. The skill needed to perform sen-sen-no-sen is of such a high degree that the beginning student is advised to first work on responding to an attack, go-no-sen, and later on moving in unison with an attack, ai-uchi. Sen-sen-no-sen takes many years to develop.

Zan-Shin

Zan-Shin means "the spirit that remains" in Japanese and encapsulates the idea that follow through is important. The word *zan* means afterwards and *shin* means heart or spirit in Japanese. The martial arts tradition of Japan places great emphasis on doing techniques with heart and spirit, and not just thinking of them in a purely physical, mechanical way. There exist many fine books detailing the spiritual aspects of the martial arts and Aikido in particular, and the reader is urged to look to them for more profound guidance about executing techniques with a great deal of spirit. For our purposes, however, it must be pointed out that the level of mental intensity and awareness that is needed to properly execute an Aikido technique must be maintained even after the mechanical parts of the technique have been completed. That is, one needs follow through. A proper golf swing does not end the moment that golf club hits the golf ball. Rather, the proper swing continues in its long arc well after the ball is flying down the fairway. In the same fashion, Aikido techniques do not end at the moment that the physical objective of the technique has been completed. Even with throwing techniques, mental intensity and concentration, and indeed bodily movement, continue well after the attacker is thrown by the defender. The reader is advised to execute techniques not only with a lot of heart and spirit, *shin*, but also to remember to continue that intensity even after the mechanical parts of the technique are completed. If she does so, the reader will have good zan-shin.

Putting it all Together

All of the basic skills listed above need to be done correctly for Aikido to work well. Before we proceed with discussing individual techniques, we will examine one single Aikido technique and use it to point out how its proper execution incorporates all the skills previously discussed.

The technique called *Shi-ho Nage* is one common to all styles of Aikido. The technique's name (which means the Four Directions Throw) derives from the fact that the defender turns through all of the four directions of the compass. The technique is illustrated in Figures 22-28 by an unarmed defender who is attacked by a man stabbing at him with a *tanto*, a Japanese dagger. (For safety, a mock knife was used.)

Figures 22–23

合氣道

In the Figure 22, the defender has established proper distance, ma-ai. He also stands properly in shizen-tai, and utilizes proper me-tsuke to look at his assailant. Note that because the defender has established ma-ai, the attacker must take a step toward the defender in order to get close enough to attempt a stab. In the Figure 23, the defender begins his tai-sabaki movement after determining that the attacker is making a committed attack and not just feigning. This tai-sabaki movement takes the defender forward and to his right. It brings him close to the attacker and puts him in a position to grab and manipulate the attacker's stabbing arm. Such a manipulation is begun in Figure 24 before the attacker has fully completed his stab. The defender grabs the wrist of the attacker's stabbing arm and then keeps his arms in front of his center line as he turns his hips, moves his center, and uses that turning force to bend the attacker's arm and break the attacker's balance. In Figure 25, the defender continues to move his feet and his whole body forward and uses that locomotive force, that ido-ryoku, to further

Figures 24–26

bend the attacker's arm and achieve very good kuzushi by pushing the attacker forward and sideways. With solid kuzushi established, the fancy turning-around part of the technique can easily be done. It begins with the defender raising his own arms straight up his center line while still grabbing the attacker's wrist in Figure 26. Once his own wrists are about forehead level, the defender turns around by pivoting on the balls of both feet simultaneously. Doing so fold's the attacker's stabbing arm at the elbow and also bends the attacker backward, as can be seen in Figure 27. Notice that throughout the turn, the defender keeps his hands in front of his center line. The mechanical part of the technique ends with the attacker bent over backwards with his stabbing arm pinned behind him. From there it is easy to take the knife away or to throw him to the ground. The latter is illustrated in Figure 28, which also shows the defender displaying good zan-shin, continuing to keep mental intensity and proper posture even after uke is thrown to the ground, by pushing forward with the whole body.

The student should study Figures 22-28 several times, and should be able to identify the use of all of the following principles by the defender: shizen-tai, ma-ai, me-tsuke, tai-sabaki, ido-ryoku, sei-chu sen, kuzushi, timing, attacking the physical weak points of the body, and zan-shin. Moreover,

Figures 27–28

合氣道

he should remember these basic principles when learning any new technique. Without them, no technique can be done correctly.

Body and Movement Terms

Before we go on to explain in great detail the proper way of doing several Aikido techniques, a few more terms and concepts describing body movement and the interaction of attacker and defender must be presented.

Tegatana

Te is the Japanese word for hand, and *gatana* is the Japanese word for sword; hence, tegatana describes a hand sword. The name is a bit misleading, however, because the word tegatana refers to the entire arm and not just the hand itself. A tegatana is shown in Figures 29–30. It is formed by an extended arm; with the elbow held stiff; with the wrist held stiff; the fingers held stiff, extended and together; and with the thumb extended and held away from the palm. Though the arm is held stiff at the elbow joint, the elbow joint is not fully extended and locked out. Rather, the tegatana arm should have the same gentle curvature as a Japanese sword.

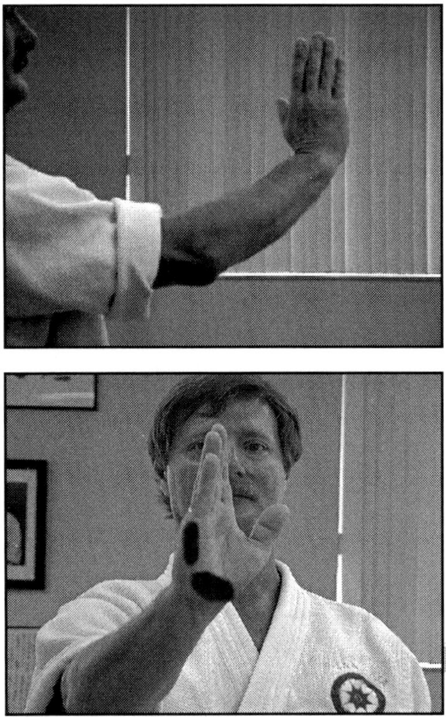

Figures 29–30

The tegatana is quite useful in aikido because its stiffness makes it the perfect lever with which to take power generated by moving one's center and utilize it to push on an uke during various techniques. Often, however, the wrong part of the hand is used to push with; practitioners incorrectly push with the edge of the hand extending from the little finger to the wrist. Pushing that way puts overly great and unnatural strain on the wrist joint. The correct areas with which pushing pressure should be applied are on the palm of the hand and are shown in the Figure 30. When an Aikido player pushes with a tegatana, no arm strength is used, as the pushing is done from the center of mass using ido-ryoku. The tegatana is just the lever through which power is applied.

It should also be noted here that a tegatana is often referred to as an "unbendable arm" by English speaking Aikido practitioners. The tegatana is indeed a very strong structure and there are many ways to demonstrate that an opponent cannot, using his own body weight and upper body strength, bend a tegatana arm at the elbow. This should, however, serve as a warning to beginners: when utilizing tegatana, it is not the other guy who will bend your arm and cause you to have poor tegatana and bad form. Rather, whenever bad form results, it is your own fault. Be sure not to let the elbow joint bend and the arm fold up when doing techniques that require a proper, fully extended tegatana. A bent arm is not only structurally weak, but makes it very difficult to push from one's center and utilize the full power of ido-ryoku.

Tsukuri versus Stepping

We will differentiate between movement of the body by means of stepping with the feet, and by means of using *tsukuri* with the feet. Stepping means ordinary walking steps. Tsukuri means moving forward by sliding the feet, with the leading foot always remaining the same. This is illustrated in Figures 31-33. The person begins with his right foot forward in the first frame. To move forward, instead of stepping forward with the left foot, he pushes off on the left foot and slides forward with the right foot always in front of the left, both feet touching the ground at all times.

Kuzushi Lines

To add to the understanding of how kuzushi will be achieved in the techniques described in this book, we must look at lines of balance. In Figure 34, the person begins standing in a right-foot-forward stance. Notice the two lines drawn on the floor in the picture. The solid line travels directly between the person's heels. The dotted line is set at a 90-degree angle to the solid line and bisects the solid line at a distance halfway between the heels. Pressures exerted along these lines will be used in the techniques presented later in this book to unbalance and achieve kuzushi.

These lines are crucial to achieving kuzushi. If the person is pulled forward along the dotted line, his balance is easily

Figures 31-33

broken if he does not move his feet, as is shown in Figure 35. Similarly, if he is pushed backward along the dotted line as in Figure 36, his balance is also easily broken if he does not move his feet. Kuzushi can also be achieved by movement along the solid line, as in Figure 37. If pressure is applied to the person's torso in the direction of the solid line, the person's weight is pushed onto a single foot, thereby breaking balance. Many Aikido techniques achieve their kuzushi by pushing the attacker along the directions of the solid and dotted lines.

There are other directions in which one can think of pushing an attacker off balance. The symbol for the Shodokan style of Aikido (Figure 38) is an eight-pointed star, representing the eight directions in which a defender can move to avoid an

Figures 34–37

attack, as well as the eight directions in which a defender can push an attacker so as to break the attacker's balance. Tomiki Sensei included the eight-pointed star in the symbol to remind his students of the eight directions. The red dot in the center represents one's inner energy, which blends with the rest of the world's energy (the white part of the symbol) by movements of the body (the blue part of the symbol) in the eight directions. A color image of the symbol can be found on the back cover of this book.

The major point to remember when utilizing lines of balance, however, is that no person can be strong along all lines of balance simultaneously. For instance, a person is much more stable along the solid line running between the heels than he is along the perpendicular dotted line in Figure 34. Consequently, it is much easier to break a person's balance if he is pushed along the dotted line rather than along the solid line. Many aikido techniques take advantage of this physiological fact by having the defender push along a balance line along which the attacker is relatively weak and easily unbalanced. However, balance breaking along the solid line also happens. The reader should pay attention when looking at the pictures of each of the techniques presented in this book to see which balance line is being used against the attacker in each technique.

Uke and Tori

The standard names for "attacker" and "defender" that we will use in the rest of this book are *uke* and *tori*. We use the Japanese term *uke* to describe the person to whom a technique is done. *Uke*

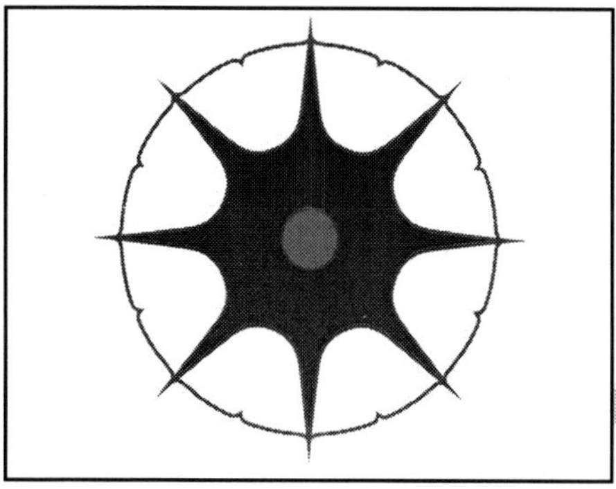

Figures 38

means receiver in Japanese. We use the term *tori* to describe the person applying the technique to uke. Tori is Japanese for doer or performer. However, since Aikido is a defensive martial art, it is usually the case that uke initiates the sequence of attack and defense. Uke first attacks and tries to do something to tori, who defends against uke's attack by applying an Aikido technique which uke then receives. In the beginner-level techniques covered in the rest of this book, uke begins the sequence of offense and defense by grabbing tori's wrist. Tori responds to uke's attack by performing an Aikido technique which either restrains or throws uke.

The 8th and 7th Kyus

In Shodokan Aikido, the curriculum is divided into logical, structured groups of techniques. Learning one group prepares you for the next group, and your progress will be quickened by practice exercises tailored to each group of techniques. After learning each group, you will be tested to see how well you are progressing. There are eight groups before black belt, all of which are called *kyu*. They count down from 8th kyu to 1st kyu. From black belt onward, the groups go by the name of *dan*, but they count up instead of down: 1st dan, 2nd dan, and so on, up to 10th dan.

The curricula of the 8th and 7th kyus are designed to teach the beginning student the basic Aikido principles of movement and interaction described previously. As all of the techniques in these kyu levels are performed against hand grabs, they can be done very slowly and without haste, allowing the student to focus on fundamentals. After the fundamentals taught by these techniques are mastered, the student can go on to deal with much faster attacks (especially knife stabs) and be expected to move properly at higher speeds.

The 8th Kyu

The three techniques of the 8th kyu are all defenses against the same attack, the cross-hand grab. The cross-hand grab involves uke reaching out with his right hand and grabbing the right wrist of tori or, conversely, uke reaching out with his left hand and grabbing the left wrist of tori. To do either, uke must reach across his own center line, an action which inspires the name cross-hand grab.

You can see this attack illustrated in Figures 39-40. Uke and tori begin standing at ma-ai in Figure 39. In Figure 40, uke attacks tori with a cross-hand grab. Note uke's footwork. As uke reaches out with his right hand to grab tori's right wrist, uke steps forward with his right foot. This is the same coordinated hand and foot movement which people use when they reach out to grab a door handle or when they reach for a salt shaker on a table top. As this is how people normally coordinate feet and hands when they go to grab something, it is also the way in which an attacker would likely coordinate feet and hands if he tried to perform a cross-hand grab when attacking.

The three techniques of the 8th kyu are *Shomen-ate*, *Oshi-taoshi*, and *Kote-gaeshi*. As you progress in your Aikido training, you will see variations of these techniques again and again, whether against punches,

Figures 39-40

合氣道

kicks, or weapons. Be sure to memorize their names now, as you will encounter these techniques over and over.

Shomen-ate

Shomen-ate means "forward strike" in Japanese. As you can see in Figures 41-50, shomen-ate received the "forward" part of its name because it involves tori moving forward to throw uke. However, there is no actual strike in the technique. The movement against uke's head and chest is executed as a push, not a punch; therefore, do not take the technique's name literally.

The technique begins with tori and uke standing at ma-ai in Figure 41. Uke then steps forward in Figure 42 to grab tori's right hand. As tori sees the grab coming, tori relaxes his hand and turns the hand so that the thumb is pointing downward by the time uke completes the grab. Next, tori begins the tai-sabaki of this technique by moving forward and to his right in Figure 43. As he does this, he begins to roll his wrist clockwise

Figure 41–43

so that the palm is facing upward. He does this keeping the hand in his center, along his sei-chu sen. As tori slides forward and to the right, he also rotates to his left along his body's vertical axis. This brings him to rest facing uke's center; tori is standing on the dotted line of Figures 34-37. This can be seen in Figure 44, where tori has completed the tai-sabaki movement and has lowered his right hand so that it is directly in front his center of mass. Lowering the hand in this way pulls uke off balance and creates kuzushi. Notice this kuzushi is just like that of Figure 35, where the person pictured is pulled forward along the dotted line.

Uke's natural reaction to being pulled forward and off balance will be to pull backwards. As uke pulls backward, tori follows the pull in toward uke, closing the distance between them in Figure 45. By Figure 46, tori has pushed in with his right arm so far that uke is again off balance, this time leaning backwards. To achieve this, tori kept his right hand relaxed and pushed it into the bend in uke's right wrist, collapsing uke's arm and pinning it against uke's chest. To

Figures 44–46

合氣道

complete the technique, tori next rotates his right hand, turning the palm towards uke as in Figure 47. Note that uke is leaned over backwards, and that tori's entire forearm is pressed up against uke's upper chest: contact is made with the entire tegatana, not just the hand part of the tegatana. Tori then throws uke in the Figures 48–50 by using ido-ryoku. Tori uses tsukuri to slide forward, and simultaneously lowers his body weight, thereby lowering his tegatana arm, and so not only pushes uke backward but downward as well. Note the correct posture and zan-shin follow through in Figure 50.

Study carefully the footwork of both uke and tori, and how tori uses his footwork to keep himself stable and centered, while unbalancing uke. As uke steps forward to

Figure 47–50

grab in Figure 42, uke is stable and balanced. For the rest of the technique, uke's feet do not move. Tori takes advantage of this in Figures 43-44 which, from uke's perspective, involve being pulled forward and to the left. When pulled that direction, uke has no foot against which to brace himself and resist the pull; as a result, uke is easily unbalanced. As uke tries to right himself by pulling backward in Figure 45, tori moves forward and pushes against uke's chest. Pushing in this direction easily breaks uke's balance because he is being pushed in a direction in which he does not have a foot against which to brace himself due to the fact that his stance has not changed since the initial attack. As tori pushes on his chin and chest in Figures 46–49, uke cannot effectively resist, as he has neither of his feet in a proper place to apply force in opposition to that being applied by tori's tegatana.

Tori makes sure that the kuzushis of Figures 43–44 and Figures 46–49 can be easily accomplished by aligning his feet correctly by Figure 44, so that they are lined up and point directly at uke's center. That is, both of tori's feet should be on the dotted line of Figure 35, with the right foot atop the dotted line and the heel of the back, left foot on the line, with the back foot turned out at a 45-degree angle to the line. By lining himself up this way, tori can apply strong ido-ryoku in a direction in which uke cannot resist. Unless uke moves his feet, the push is guaranteed to knock him over.

Finally, note the correct arm movements used by tori. At no time does he bend his elbow while performing the technique. When he is grabbed in Figure 42, his arm is relaxed and extended. As tori rotates the hand in Figures 43–44, he does so by turning the wrist over; the elbow remains extended and the arm stays relaxed. When uke pulls back and tori enters in Figures 45–46, tori stiffens his arm into a tegatana, so as to create a good pushing tool. No pushing is done with arm extension; the push comes from moving forward with the entire body, using ido-ryoku. In Figure 43–44, when tori rotates the wrist, the elbow does not bend. And again, when the throw is executed, the arm stays fully extended, and pushing is done by body movement channeled through the tegatana.

Oshi-taoshi

Oshi means pushing in Japanese, and *taoshi* means falling over or toppling. In this technique, tori pushes on uke such that uke has no choice but to fall over. Please examine Figures 51–60.

Uke and tori begin at ma-ai in the Figure 51. Uke attacks tori's right wrist with a cross-hand grab in Figure 52. As uke reaches in to grab him, tori stiffens his right arm into a tegatana and turns the hand so that the thumb faces the floor. Tori then draws back the right arm that uke is trying to grab. This achieves kuzushi and unbalances uke in Figure 53 by requiring uke to overextend himself and bend over to reach his goal of grabbing tori's wrist.

Uke will naturally try to restore his broken balance by pulling backwards in order to stand up straight again. As uke

Figures 51–53

pulls backwards, tori enters in Figures 54–56. Tori does this by sliding forward and to his right, keeping his right hand in his sei-chu sen. As tori moves forward, he turns over his tegatana by rotating his forearm, turning it over clockwise. This motion can be seen in Figures 54–55. The motion of tori's right hand turning over bends uke's right elbow and causes uke's right arm to rotate and rise. This exposes the underside of uke's arm. Tori takes advantage of this in Figure 56 by bringing his left arm up as a tegatana and pushing on uke's right arm from underneath, between the armpit and the elbow joint, next to the elbow joint. This action achieves significant kuzushi, as uke's weight is pushed onto his back, left foot. This is the same kuzushi as in Figure 37, where force was applied parallel to the

Figures 54–57

solid line. As the left hand pushes up on uke's arm, tori's right hand grabs uke's arm just above the wrist. Uke's arm is therefore controlled securely, being grabbed at the wrist and pushed up from underneath near the elbow joint.

To knock uke over and finish the technique, tori now steps forward with his left foot in Figure 57. Note that in Figures 45–56, tori maintained a right-foot-forward stance, meaning that his left foot was back and waiting to be used for the step forward of Figure 57. The forward impetus of the step is channeled through tori's stiff left tegatana arm, and provides the force needed to push uke over. Note that as tori steps forward with his left leg, he steps in front of uke and is so close to him that their hips touch. Consequently, there is a natural hip check as uke pushes into tori, and this hip check helps to transfer some of the stepping energy that knocks uke over. The hip check knocks uke sideways and to his own left, while the pressure on the arm pushes forward and down. It should also be noted that pressure is always applied to the underside of uke's arm. This technique does not rely on putting pressure on a locked elbow joint.

Finally, note that for the technique to work properly, tori must push uke's right elbow towards uke's right ear. Pushing in this direction ensures that uke cannot recover from the fall because his weight is all on his left foot and because the hip check prevents him from spinning around and attempting to use his right leg for support. Also very important is that pushing in this direction will cause uke to shoot out his left arm and use it for support as he is being pushed over. See Figure 57. This is good for tori because as long as uke's left hand is on the ground, uke cannot use it to grab or punch tori.

As uke falls, his right arm naturally extends out with the elbow locking. As uke falls and the arm locks out, tori applies an elbow pin to keep uke's elbow locked. Tori does this by pinning his own right hand (which, recall, is gripping uke's forearm just above the wrist) against his right hipbone. The left tegatana hand then keeps slight downward pressure on uke's elbow so that uke cannot bend his arm and get up.

Because tori took a big step with his left foot to knock uke over in Figure 57, he is now in a left-foot-forward stance with his left leg flush against the right side of uke's rib cage. Were the technique to end here with this pin, things would be precarious for tori, as uke could attempt to pick his left hand off the mat and grab tori's left leg. This is dangerous for tori. To move into a safer position, tori tsukuris forward and to the left, pushing his left hipbone in the direction of uke's left shoulder. This causes uke to sprawl forward in Figure 58 and place his left hand on the floor where it is occupied and unable to punch or grab tori. As he is being pushed, uke's torso often rotates away from tori as seen in Figure 58.

This game of tsukuri-ing forward and to the left to keep tori sprawled forward and putting his left hand on the floor cannot continue indefinitely. For the final pin, tori switches his

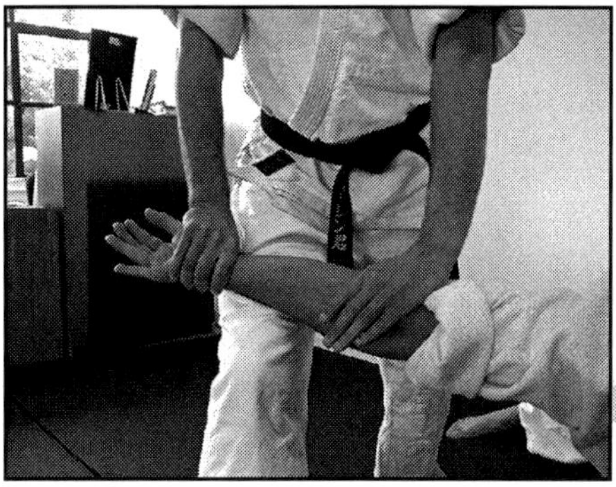

Figures 58–60

合氣道

stance from left-foot forward to right-foot forward. This moves tori's left leg out of grabbing distance of uke's left hand. This is done in Figure 59. Keeping the left foot where it is, tori takes a sliding step forward with the right foot (keeping uke's wrist pinned against tori's right hip) and then keeping the right foot where it is pulls his left foot backward and away from uke's torso. Stepping forward with the right leg locks up uke's shoulder joint. Pulling the left leg away from uke's torso puts that leg beyond uke's reach. In taking the two steps, tori rotates his center about 30 degrees counterclockwise if the action is viewed from directly above.

As a final step, tori slides his right hand down his own right thigh. Since his right hand is grabbing uke's locked arm, this moves uke's arm into its final position. The pin which finishes the technique involves tori holding uke's right wrist on his own right knee while keeping his left tegatana over uke's locked right elbow. The tegatana over uke's elbow should be in tori's sei-chu sen, so that if uke tries to raise up, tori can just sink his body weight down on the elbow, without the need to utilize any upper body strength to maintain the pin.

The correct hand positions are shown in Figure 60. Tori's right hand is on the outside of tori's right knee, and, while grabbing uke's wrist, tori's own right wrist is bent back so that the palm of that right hand is parallel to the floor. This is because if uke tries to pull his arm toward his own torso, he will have to pull against tori's entire right leg, as the correct grip braces uke's grabbing hand on the far side of tori's right leg so that that leg can be used for support.

Kote-gaeshi

Kote is the Japanese term for the heel of the hand or the base of the palm. *Gaeshi* means to twist back. Kote-gaeshi is a wrist-lock technique in which the small of the hand is grabbed and twisted to break uke's balance and throw him to the ground. See Figures 61–75.

Uke and tori begin at ma-ai in Figure 61. Uke attacks tori with a cross-hand grab in Figure 62. As the grabbing hand is approaching, tori makes his right hand into a tegatana, and rotates it so that the palm is facing upward by the time the grab is completed. Just before the grab is completed, tori slides his right foot backward, so that he is standing in a left-foot forward stance. Then, as shown in Figure 63, tori twist his hips to his own right, pivoting on the balls of his feet, keeping his right hand in his center. As he twists his torso, he rotates his tegatana hand counterclockwise so that the palm turns over to face the floor. This combined body and hand twisting breaks uke's balance, lowering uke's right shoulder and pulling uke forward. However, uke's balance can be broken even more. To

Figures 61–64

accomplish this, tori twists his hips a full 180 degrees and then takes a lunging tsukuri, lowering his center by bending the knees while pushing forward with the feet. This is illustrated in Figure 64. As he performs the lunging tsukuri, tori pushes his right tegatana hand toward his own right knee. The combination of the lunging tsukuri and the pushing with the tegatana creates a very complete kuzushi.

Note that in Figures 62-64, tori never grabs uke's right arm with his right hand. Rather, tori's right hand is kept in a tegatana. This is done for two reasons. The first is that it is much easier to push on uke with a tegatana rather than a grabbing hand. Second, it gives tori's left hand more access to uke's wrist as the technique subsequently develops. When tori pushes uke's arm towards his own right knee, he pushes with a tegatana, as seen in Figure 64. By not grabbing uke with the right hand, tori can slide his left hand underneath the right tegatana and grab the base of uke's right wrist. This grab is made during the lunging tsukuri

Figure 65–67

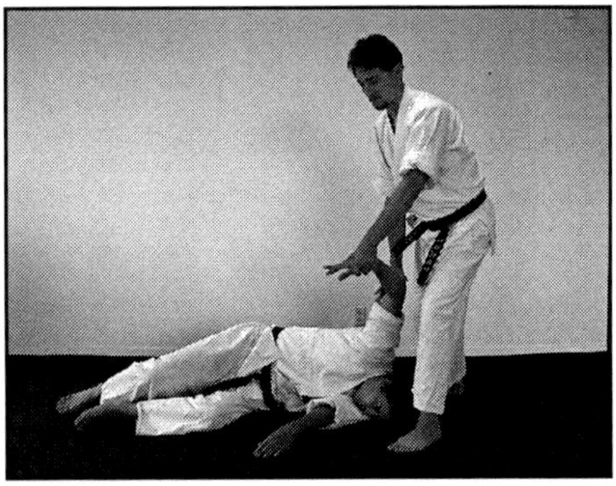

and can be seen both in Figure 64 and in the close up of Figure 73.

With his balance completely broken, uke will try to recover by standing up. As uke begins to rise in Figure 65 tori does not hinder uke. Rather, tori prepares to take advantage of uke's rising. Tori steps behind himself with his left leg and begins to pivot on the right foot toward his own left. As tori does this, he simultaneously begins breaking uke's grip on his arm by sliding his right tegatana towards the left, across his body. With uke's arm being held tightly by his left hand, this leftward motion with the right tegatana causes uke's wrist to buckle and fold, releasing uke's grip on tori's arm and locking uke's wrist. At the end of this grip breaking, tori's forearm comes to rest on the back of

Figures 68–71

uke's hand as seen in Figure 67, and in the close ups of Figures 73-75. Note that throughout this grip-breaking process, tori has continued to keep his hands in his center as he rotates his body to the left by pivoting on the ball of the right foot. It is crucial to understand that the pressure that tori needs to apply to break uke's grip comes not from upper body strength but from the energy of tori's spinning torso.

Tori next throws uke by simultaneously pushing down on the back of uke's right hand with his right forearm while continuing to twist to his own left. This is illustrated in Figures 68–69. Note that as uke twists his body to generate the force needed to throw uke, he keeps his hands in his own sei-chu sen. The rotational power of tori spinning his torso pulls uke forward and off balance. Uke is forced to either fall sideways or take a forward break fall.

A pin to the wrist completes the technique. After falling down, uke is on his back, as in Figure 69. Tori's left hand still holds uke's right wrist. Tori stiffens his right hand into a tegatana and uses it to push on the inside of uke's elbow, the side that would face uke's chest if uke were standing up normally with his arms dangling by his side. Tori presses in the direction of uke's head, as shown in Figures 69–70. This pressure causes uke's torso to rotate. Uke turns toward his own left side and onto his belly. As uke rolls over, tori maintains his grip with the left hand and walks around uke's head, ending up in a left-foot-forward stance. Tori first steps forward and to the left in Figure 70, and then pivots on the forward left foot. He pivots back and to his right in Figure 71. Viewed from above, tori is rotating clockwise. By the time uke rolls over completely, tori has turned 180 degrees, and is facing uke's head, as in Figure 72.

Tori pins uke using uke's right wrist, which tori is still grabbing with his left hand. Tori places his entire left forearm along the length of his left thigh, with the back of the forearm and the back of the hand facing the thigh. Tori bends his own left wrist so that it drapes over the bend in his left knee, with the back of the left hand draping down toward the foreleg. This can be seen in Figure 72. Tori finally leans forward by bending the left knee. Doing so puts a great deal of pressure on uke's bent arm, pinning uke to the floor and putting him in a fair amount of pain. This pin completes the technique.

Figures 73–75 give a close up view of the grip break used in Figures 64–67. Tori's left hand holds uke's arm still while tori's right tegatana pushes across to break uke's grip and pin uke's wrist backwards.

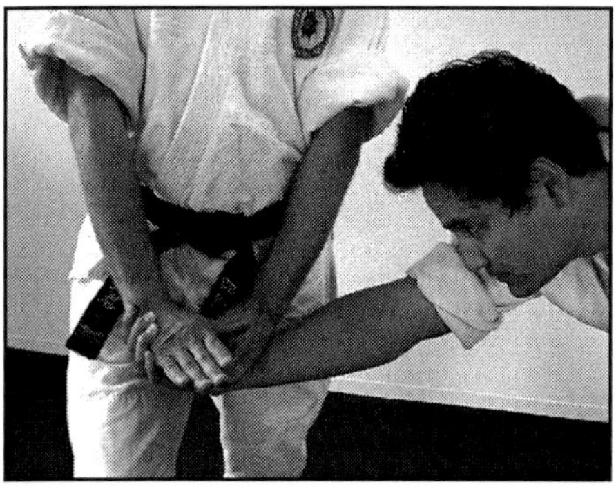

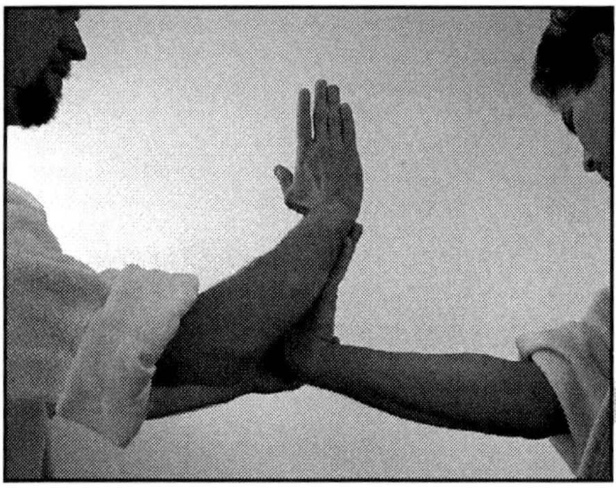

Figures 72–75

The 7th Kyu

The three techniques of the 7th kyu are performed against one-handed same-side grabs. The one-handed same-side grab involves uke stepping forward with his right foot and grabbing tori's left hand with his own right hand; or uke stepping forward with his left foot and grabbing tori's right hand with his own left hand. As with the cross-hand grab studied above, the hands and feet move together, with the right foot stepping forward when the right hand goes to grab, and vice versa. See Figures 76-77 for an example of uke performing a same-side grab. Uke uses his own right hand to grab tori's left hand.

The three 7th kyu techniques are ai-gamae ate, hiki-taoshi, and tenkai kote-hineri. As with the 8th kyu techniques, learn these names now.

Ai-gamae ate

Gamae is the Japanese word for stance or stances. The word *ai* used in the name of this technique is the same as the "ai" in Aikido, and means matching. The word *ate* used in the name of this technique means strike, and is the same as the "ate" in shomen-ate. Thus, the name of this technique translates as the matching stances strike. As with shomen-ate, however, the

Figure 76–77

合氣道

"strike" involved is actually a push. Uke should not be punched while performing the technique, which actually involves pulling uke laterally off balance and then pushing him over as in Figures 78–84.

Uke and tori begin at ma-ai in Figure 78. Uke uses his right hand and attacks tori's left hand with a same-side grab in Figure 79. Just before the grab is completed, tori makes his left hand into a tegatana, and positions the tegatana so that the palm is facing the floor and the fingers are pointing forward and to tori's right. This is seen in Figure 80.

Tori keeps his grabbed left wrist and tegatana in front of his left hip as he slides his feet and moves to his own left and forward in Figure 81. As tori tsukuris, he leads with his left leg and finishes the slide in a left-foot-forward stance. By the time this motion is completed, uke has been pulled off balance to his right and backwards. This kuzushi is essential for the technique to work, and is accomplished by tori pushing uke off balance using ido-ryoku;

Figures 78–80

tori does not try to drag uke off balance by using the muscular strength of his left arm. The proper kuzushi is shown in Figure 82, which is out of sequence and is what Figure 81 would look like if the camera were placed behind uke's head.

While tori is pushing uke off balance by sliding forward and channeling that energy through his left tegatana arm, his right arm swings forward from the shoulder as a tegatana and comes up to push on the left side of uke's face. This is seen in Figures 80-82. Pressure is applied with the tegatana to the underside of uke's jaw so that uke's neck twists to uke's right. Tori places the palm of the right hand under uke's left jaw bone so that the palm is flush against the jaw. Tori then flips that right hand over to twist uke's head sideways. The

Figure 81–84

turning of uke's head bends uke's neck and upper spine, adding to the kuzushi achieved by using ido-ryoku when sliding forward and to the left.

Tori next uses his right tegatana to throw uke before uke can regain his balance. Tori steps forward with his right leg and directs the resulting stepping energy through his right tegatana to throw uke in Figures 83-84. The direction of the push used to throw is important. The step is taken toward a spot behind uke's left heel. The step is executed so that tori's right foot steps behind uke's torso, as shown in Figure 83. Uke is forced backwards and to his left and takes a back fall in Figure 84. As the step is taken, tori's torso is flush with uke's and there should be a gentle hip check as the bodies come together. This hip check transfers some of the energy of tori's forward step, and helps to throw uke. Additionally, the hip check throws uke's lower body sideways and prevents uke from stepping backward to regain his balance.

The name of this technique, ai-gamae ate, derives from the stances of uke and tori just as the technique is ending. Just as the throw is being made, both uke and tori are in right-foot-forward stances; that is, they have ai-gamae or matching stances.

Hiki-taoshi

Hiki means pulling in Japanese. The word *taoshi* here is the same as the *taoshi* in oshi-taoshi and means falling over or toppling. *Hiki-taoshi* involves tori pushing on uke's bent arm so that uke has no choice but to fall down, as illustrated in Figures 85–93.

Uke and tori start out in Figure 85 at ma-ai. In Figure 86, uke begins his same-side grab of tori's left wrist. Just before the grab is completed in Figure 87, tori makes his left hand into a tegatana and rotates it so that the palm faces upwardward and the thumb points left.

Tori next relaxes the left tegatana hand and grabs uke's right forearm. At the same time, tori reaches up with his right hand and grabs uke's grabbing right hand from above. This sandwiches uke's hand between tori's left forearm and tori's right hand. While both of tori's hands are grabbing uke's arm, tori begins to rotate uke's arm. This can be seen in Figure 88, where, from tori's perspective, the hands are rotating clockwise.

Continuing to rotate tori's arm in this fashion, tori steps forward with his right foot, placing it directly in front of uke's center in Figure 89. Using the momentum of this step forward, tori pushes uke's right hand towards uke's chin. Rotating uke's arm causes both the elbow and the wrist joints to bend and the arm to collapse. This is very advantageous to tori because tori is pushing into uke with two straight arms while uke can only resist using one collapsed arm.

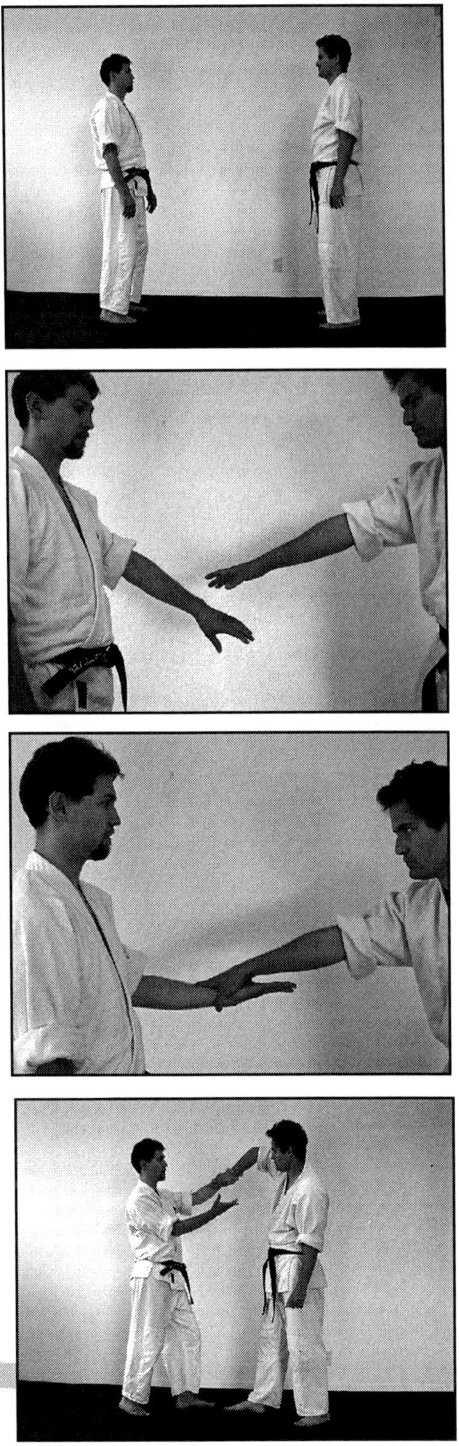

Figure 85–88

The forward momentum of the tsukuri combined with the rotation of the hands not only bends uke's elbow but also leans uke backward, breaking his balance. Uke attempts to lean forward to regain his balance. As he does, tori pivots to his left on the ball of his forward, right foot. Tori pivots just enough so that his heels both come to rest on the dashed kuzushi line of Figures 34-37. Doing this puts tori in an excellent position to break uke's balance by pushing backwards along the dashed line. This pulls uke forward and off balance using the same kuzushi as was illustrated in Figure 35.

To do this, tori first pulls his hands down into his center as in Figure 90. Among other things, this fully extends uke's arm and locks out uke's right elbow. Then, keeping his hands in his center, tori pushes backwards using his forward, right foot. To uke, this feels like he is being pulled forward along his dashed kuzushi line. The pull, if done precisely, will compel uke to fall forward and will also cause uke to try to catch himself by reaching forward his left hand as can be

Figures 89–91

seen in Figure 91. As uke is falling forward, tori places his right hand as a tegatana behind and above uke's right elbow. This ensures that uke's arm will remain locked up at the elbow joint and will prevent uke from attempting to rise up by bending the elbow.

Tori continues to push backward with his forward, right foot until uke falls forward onto his belly as in Figure 92. A simple arm bar pin completes the technique. Tori places his forward, right foot under uke's right collarbone, keeps uke's arm fully extended, and maintains his own right tegatana hand above uke's locked-out elbow joint to prevent uke from rising. This can be seen in both Figure 92 as well as in Figure 93, which is a reverse-angle shot of the same pin.

Tenkai Kote-hineri

Tenkai is a Japanese word meaning to spin around. *Kote* means the small of the hand and is the same "kote" as in kote-gaeshi. *Hineri* is a word that means twisting. The name of this technique comes from the fact that tori spins his whole body around to get the leverage needed to lock up uke's wrist by twisting the small of the hand, as can be seen in Figures 94-107.

Uke and tori begin at ma-ai in Figure 94. Uke reaches

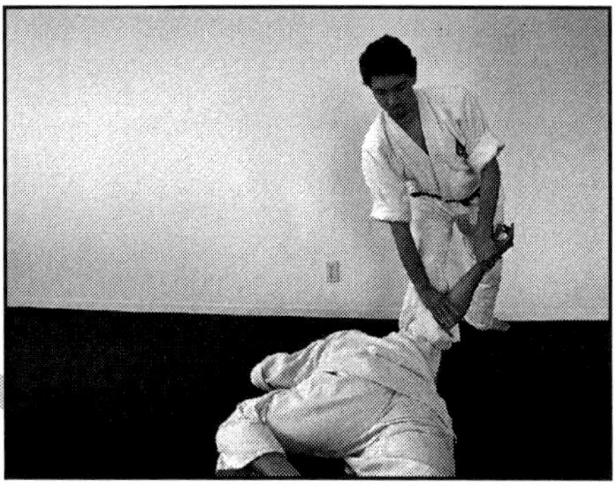

Figure 92–93

合氣道

forward with his right hand to grab tori's left hand in Figure 95. Just before the grab is completed, tori stiffens his left arm into a tegatana and rotates his left hand blade so that the blade faces the floor. As the grab is completed, tori begins to tsukuri forward and to the left, leading with the left foot, as shown in Figure 96. Tori channels the momentum of that tsukuri through his left tegatana arm and uses it to push uke off balance, back and to the right from uke's persepective. A subtle point is that as tori is pushing forward with the left tegatana, he rotates it clockwise so that the palm faces the floor. This allows tori to push with the base of the palm and channel his energy well. Additionally, the rotation of tori's wrist also rotates uke's wrist into a weak configuration.

At the same time that tori is using tsukuri to go forward and the left, tori brings his right arm up as a tegatana and places it palm up on the under side of uke's jaw, on the left side of uke's face, as in Figure 96. Tori then turns his right tegatana hand over counter clockwise

Figures 94–96

(from tori's perspective) and pushes uke's head back and to the right (from uke's perspective) in Figure 97. By doing this, tori can channel the momentum of his tsukuri through both arms and push uke off balance. *As the reader will notice, this technique is so far identical to the beginning parts of ai-gamae ate,* and is equivalent to Figures 78–81. Unlike ai-gamae ate, which continues into a throw after this two-tegatana kuzushi is achieved, tenkai-kote hineri uses this kuzushi to unbalance uke long enough that tori can safely apply the joint lock that gives this technique its name.

After pushing uke's jaw with his right tegatana, tori lowers his right arm and uses his right hand to grab uke's right forearm just above the wrist in Figure 98. In properly executing the rest of the technique, tori's elbows remain extended and his hands stay in front of his sei-chu sen.

The kuzushi achieved by tsukuri-ing forward and to the left in Figures 96–98 not only pulls uke slightly off balance, but raises his arm upwards so that tori may spin under it to complete the technique. He does

Figures 97–99

this by first stepping forward with his right foot in Figure 99. This step brings tori's right shoulder next to uke's arm pit. Tori next raises his own tegatana arms vertically up his center line, raising the arms by rotating at the shoulder joint (tori does NOT bend his elbows). By raising his own arms in Figure 100, tori will also raise uke's right arm, and open up enough space so that tori can pivot 180 degrees on the balls of both feet, rotating toward his own left as in Figure 101. Notice that as he rotates, tori keeps his hands in his center. This 180-degree rotation locks up uke's wrist as in Figure 102. The wrist lock should be applied with enough force that it is painful and uke rises up onto his toes as he attempts to relieve the pressure.

Figures 100–102

Tori now breaks uke's grip on his left hand. Tori does this by pulling his left tegatana hand toward his own chest, parallel to the floor as in Figure 103. Pulling in this direction puts force on the thumb of uke's right hand, a force which will be too much for the thumb by itself to resist. After freeing his left hand in this way, tori uses the left hand to grab uke's right hand from above using a pistol grip, as shown in Figure 104. This wrist lock should be maintained firmly, and should, as before, be painful enough that uke rises up onto his toes in an attempt to relieve the pressure. Uke's being up on his toes is a form of kuzushi, and uke will be too unstable up on his toes to mount an effective resistance.

Note that after turning around in Figures 99–101, tori is standing in a left-foot forward stance which is maintained through Figure 104. To pin uke to the ground and complete the technique, tori first steps forward with his right foot in Figure 105 and channels the energy of the step through his left tegatana, using it to push uke forward and down. Tori next pivots to the left on the ball of his right foot, sliding his left foot behind himself, as in Figure 106. Viewed from above, this would be a counterclockwise pivot. The pivot motion is nearly 180 degrees, so that uke and tori almost face each other by the end of the movement. As the pivot is completed in Figure 106,

Figures 103–105

uke's arm naturally extends, but tori keeps it slightly bent by applying downward pressure with his right tegatana on the bent underside of the elbow. Tori does not allow the elbow to lock out. Notice that at this point, uke's balance is severely broken. To force uke onto his belly, tori simply tsukuris backwards, pushing with his right foot and maintaining a right-foot forward stance as he does so.

To pin uke and complete the technique in Figure 107, tori places his right foot just under uke's right shoulder while keeping uke's right arm fully extended at the elbow. Tori then uses his right tegatana to put downward pressure on uke's locked right elbow while simultaneously bending his right knee and pressing with his right shin upon uke's arm. Both pressures serve to pin uke's arm. However, a more subtle point is that tori never releases the kote-hineri wrist lock that he achieves in Figure 104. As uke is pinned in Figure 107, tori continues to crank firmly on uke's right wrist with the joint lock. The result of this cranking is that uke's shoulder joint locks up and the shoulder is pinned securely to the floor by the torque applied to the wrist.

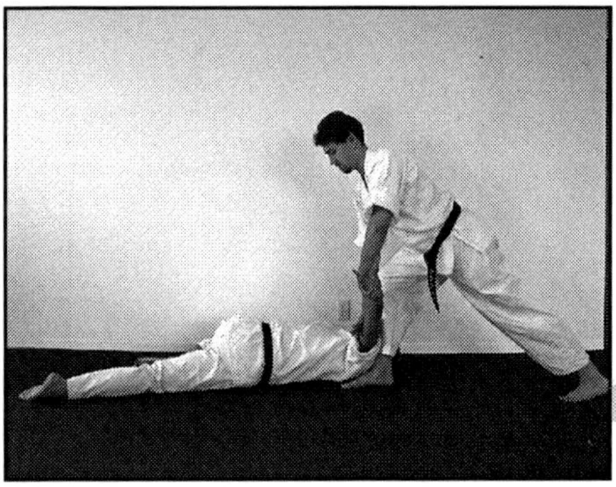

Figures 106–107

Conclusion

This volume was designed to present the basic concepts of Shodokan Aikido in an integrated and unified form, giving detailed presentations of not only the general movements of techniques, but a few of the unifying principles and subtle points as well. It is the author's hope, however, that readers will seek out a good sensei so that they can learn for themselves the many dozens of subtle points required to do each technique optimally. It is said that a picture is worth a thousand words. In the same way, a technique learned directly is worth a thousand photos in a martial arts book.

However, noting that Aikido is subtle and difficult to learn is not meant to discourage readers. Aikido is a treasure chest of knowledge about human physiology, applied physics, psychology, and the most basic intuitions of what it is to be a person and live as a human being. The proper student of Aikido takes time to admire each of these treasures and comes to see technique and practice as merely being the keys to unlock the treasure chest that is Aikido. A person may begin to study Aikido in order to learn techniques, but he continues as he realizes that Aikido teaches him about his place in the world, and about his fellow men and how to deal with them justly and compassionately.

It is hoped that this book will aid many to grasp a first understanding of the techniques of Aikido. But the author will not be satisfied if the reader merely learns techniques. The true end of the Warrior Path is not technique. Rather, it is understanding: understanding of self, of others, and of the proper life of man in this world. If this book helps even a few toward that true end, the author will be well pleased.

Index

合氣道